THE RED TIE BLUES

Celebrating the End of the Trump Reign

R.C.

Contents

THE RED TIE BLUES

Introduction

Feeling politically impotent, I resort to signing petitions, writing to senators, and submitting letters to the editor. These acts make me feel better, temporarily, but that is not what I am after. I would like those in power to pay attention to those they serve. Pretty simple; rarely effected.

The reasonable request for President Trump to release his tax returns has taken the form of a petition, which I signed, and which you can sign at the website petitions.whitehouse.gov. The website is emblazoned with hopeful language: "We the People," and "Your voice in the White House." At last count, one month after the inauguration, well over one million people had signed—giving the lie to Trump's statement that no one except journalists is interested in his tax filings.

Will Trump's White House listen? Doubtful. Let's see how long the site remains up and running. Trump clearly resents messages he can't control. Witness his reaction to comparisons between the size of crowds at his, versus Obama's, inauguration. One was much smaller than the other. Witness his rants at the media. Witness his wiretapping fantasies. Witness that damn red tie. Trump! Ditch the tie!

On occasion I write to senators, seeking to spark some thought, or at least a recognition that citizens' opinions should be taken into account when a senator develops a position on this or that issue.

Do I hear back? Sometimes, but always in the form of a form letter about this or that position, never a personalized note. Are my messages read by staffers? By senators? By some sort of computer code? Who knows?

I also write, now and then, to the editor of "failing" newspapers, in support of their mission to keep political malfeasance in front of the public—but also in support of a longstanding American tradition of ridiculing those in power who deserve to be ridiculed.

Dear Editor,

The lovely adjective "twitterpated," made popular for a time by the 1940s Disney film Bambi, refers to being infatuated or obsessed. The Urban Dictionary defines it as a state of being completely enamored with someone or something. Whatever one makes of Disney cartoons, or indeed of cartoonish political figures, we need a noun to describe a tweeting president. Perhaps Twitterpater-in-Chief, or President Twitterpater, captures the inanity of the phenomenon and the quality of the personality.

Who listens to the random citizen out in the world? Not presidents, not senators, and not editors of grand newspapers.

Perhaps our collective voice is our only recourse, when we are otherwise ignored as individuals. The Women's March on Washington, which became a national, and indeed a world-wide, phenomenon, should at least have caused Trump to peek out of the White House windows and see a world that is not, and will never be, his creation. The one million signatures on the White House petition signifies the same fact, which bears repeating: the world is our collective creation; it is not Trump's to do with as he impulsively pleases. For reasons that mystify many of us, he continues to privilege his impulses above reality. He is clearly twitterpated with himself.

The following poems and songs are my responses to feeling politically impotent, and fall, I hope, in the tradition of ridiculing those in power who deserve our ridicule. They are part of the outpouring of disbelief at those we've placed in power. I also hate that tie.

The Red Tie Blues

His ties, in particular, have had remarkable resonance with buyers in emulating the Trump style.

—Trump.com

I got the Red Tie Blues
Kick off my shoes
Turn on the Telly
And there ain't good news
The oaf in office
Is at it again
Tweets and tweets
And there ain't no end
In sight, oh Lord, no end
In sight.

(Refrain)
He thinks he's splendid
Don't know why
Must be that damn red tie
A Windsor knot
Then it flows down his belly
Over his buckle
And hides his little nelly
Oh my, oh my, oh my.

4

He gave us all a chuckle

When he was a fool

Yeah, he's rich, still a fool

Now he's in power

We know what to do

Vote him out of office

Send him back to his tower

Oh Lord, back to his tower.

(Refrain)

He thinks he's splendid

Don't know why

Must be that damn red tie

A Windsor knot

Then it flows down his belly

Over his buckle

And hides his little nelly

Oh my, oh my, oh my.

I got the Red Tie Blues

Nothin to lose

Call up my senator

Express my views

Ya know what he tells me

Nothin at all

Doesn't have the courtesy

Return my call

Oh Lord, return my call.

(Refrain)

He thinks he's splendid

Don't know why

Must be that damn red tie

A Windsor knot

Then it flows down his belly

Over his buckle

And hides his little nelly

Oh my, oh my, oh my.

I got the Red Tie Blues

Take all my cues

From Saturday pundits

Yeah, Scooby doos

Talkin heads babble

Talkin heads abound

Talkin and a-talkin

Have'ta turn off the sound

Oh Lord, turn off that sound.

(Refrain)

He thinks he's splendid

Don't know why

Must be that damn red tie
A Windsor knot
Then it flows down his belly
Over his buckle
And hides his little nelly
Oh my, oh my, oh my.

We sure picked a winner
Likes golf 'n' self-promotion
Expensive dinners
Lots of self-devotion
Foreign policy—uh-uh
Can't be bothered
Prefers bluster
To diplomacy
Such misery
Oh Lord, such misery.

(Refrain)
He thinks he's splendid
Don't know why
Must be that damn red tie
A Windsor knot
Then it flows down his belly
Over his buckle
And hides his little nelly

Oh my, oh my, oh my.

I got the Red Tie Blues

Kick off my shoes

Turn off the Telly

There ain't good news

The oaf in office

Is at it again

Tweets and tweets

And there ain't no end

In sight, oh Lord,

No end in sight.

Tweets and Twats

And when you're a star, they let you do it. You can do anything. Grab
them by the pussy. You can do anything.

—Donald J. Trump

I

He tweets and grabs twat,
our esteemed *presidente*—
small fingered, or not,
he's caught en flagrante
delicto 'neath flared skirts.
He bleats—he's aroused
a nuclear fear and averts
his eyes, his smirk housed
surprise, his sneer a disguise
to hide from fox, from cable,
from all three of his wives,
the simplest of facts:
He is learning disabled.

II

He tweets and grabs twat,
our vulgar *presidente*—
misdirection so fraught
he flies wingéd protégés
nonstop through the night:

9

he bleats—and armored
roaches from somewhere alt-right
fear humans transgendered—
or Muslims—all banned—
and Anglos leer as one body
accoutrement of the damned:
head scarf or loose nether nose;
red necktie, withal: manly man's clothes.

III

He tweets and grabs twat,
our loser *presidente*—
his fans, happily besotted,
guffaw at his foes: émigré
Mexican outlaws, those. Sad lessons!
he bleats—No sweetheart or kin
among them! On Bannon! On Sessions!
Patriots all! On Vladimir Putin!
Lock up that wall!—Gnashing of teeth
in the gibbering void, goatish, fetid
electoral humanoid, what's beneath
the ranting, those thoughts curiously blended?
Who knows. Who cares. The tweet storm has ended.

IV

He tweets and grabs twat,

our impeached *presidente*—

naked, just so, he fled to his yacht

Secret Service in tow, naiveté

and fake news, du jour and jejune.

He bleats—I'm unique! None better!

All lies! The world spits cartoons

in reply, and comics move on: whatever.

Power thus shifts, forces unleashed,

the right growls, the left grumbles,

while Congress abides, unbowed and un-humbled.

But hey, you there in waiting, Pence—Capiche?

No more crazies in office smoking Swedish hashish.

"The gnashing of teeth in the gibbering void," is a line from Bertolt Bretch's libretto in The Seven Deadly Sins.

Hail (to the Chief)

Hail to the Chief!—what could this possibly mean
when the Chief is aught but a tweeting machine?
Lil' Marco knew best, go-slow Jeb knew better,
while at Christie's behest (his umbrage unfettered)
belt buckles were loosened and tongues wagged
in castrati unison a rock 'n' roll chorus of shagged
Democrats. A joyful noise it was not. The Lord
spat out his discomfort, poised to disown untoward
politicians, preferring penguins and dust mites
to the long-ruined towers on the Christian right,
whose dumbfounded Cruz let forth such a wail
of indignation that, amused, God himself sailed
off.

Hail the best and the brightest—yup, that's them,
crabbed Republicans singing raucous Dem-
hating songs of repeal and replace, alternative
facts the new coin of the realm, their hortative
zeal unzipped and untraceable, as *les
fonctionnaires*, lips swollen with desire, convey
loving truths and more: spongy agency air kisses
for the press to adore. The president hisses
his dissatisfaction. Nail-sick servants ignore
threats of demise, take action and score

coups of their own, as each prized pretender

to the throne, exposed and undone, saunters

away.

Hail young humans—next up in the queue:

Generational wisdom resides in forsaking those few

geezers—rank zealots, all—unwilling to see the world

before them. Cultures swirl; as winds they eddy and purl

across the planet, and our lives are transformed. Yet a born

again senate—a doddering congress tweet-heavy with scorn—

mistakes its ensorcelled spells of disaster for wise prescience.

Political mystics with depravity intact, they fail governance

and enact rituals of exclusion, head-scratching acts of spin

and avoidable blunder. Our relatives—an embarrassment of kin—

speak in thunderous tongues and drunkenly wade

in the inflatable pool, trousers rolled, as we pray they all fade

out.

The Ryan

Ryan, Ryan not alt-right
Enough to win the political fight
Of his life, of his creed
Republican spirit, not in deed.

Tear apart the safety net
Leave all students deep in debt
That's control, that's the stuff
Bernie Sanders: call his bluff.

Attend to that of little care
Health insurance do foreswear
Kiss the ring of him in power
Assume the rightful pose and cower!

What the deadlock? What the claim?
Poor people are themselves to blame!
They buy iPhones not healthcare
And pay more attention to their hair!

When the Trump threw down his tweets
And startled the press with his bleats
Did he smile his work to see?
Did he who wooed the voters woo thee?

Ryan, Ryan not alt-right
Enough to win the political fight
Of his life, of his creed
Republican spirit, not in deed.

Branded

The stars have all aligned. I think our brand is the hottest it has
ever been.

—Eric Trump

Dear Dad:

We enlisted Kellyanne Conway to cheer on Americans
with exhortations to buy (no pressure there) Ivanka's
brand of fashionable hot underwear or some such con—
The spectacular ensued: stars aligned, and our guffaws
loudly sounded around the planet—and what a treat is in store
for those born every minute, as our brand comes to rule
their choices. Steaks and vodka, jewelry and more
clothing than they could wear (the misaligned school
we must forbear, Trump University paid out a sum
of twenty five million, *that* con undone), and hotels
triumphant. We Trumps do not despair but numb
the masses with tweets and fake news and cheap zinfandel.

Dear Son:

Avoid taxes and let the Trump brand run rampant—
smile and lie as you may and gather the clan to float
gleefully above the fray in our tower encampment;
circle all Trumps in one place and let's gloat
at the unlikely outcome of the presidential race,
the vast fortunes to assemble. Conflicts? Bah!

Nothing conflictual, nothing unseemly, money hastens
money, obvious to all, of course we Trumps see no flaw
in that reasoning: I'm in power, let's all take advantage
and heat up our brand, double our green fees, travel
at taxpayer expense (that's what they're for) petty outrage
be damned: the little people, one and all, adore our dazzle.

Dear CNN:
Our brand is the hottest it has ever been
And you are all invited to enrich our kin.

Wiretapped

How low has President Obama gone to tapp [sic] my phones during the very sacred election process. This is Nixon/Watergate. Bad (or sick) guy!

—Donald J. Trump

New York loves its wiretapped tower
Whose occupant—not long in power—
Offered no proof, twittering goof,
Scorning legions of citizen doubters.

Are microwaves capable of treason?
Apparently so in this post-factual season;
The Chief so proclaims—Obama's to blame—
And his staffers all scramble to please him.

Then FBI Director James B. Comey
Unleashed his undercover homeys;
They found not a trace, DT disgraced,
Hiding ties to nefarious commies.

To distract DT leaked an old tax form—
He paid, contradicting his family's norm,
At least long ago, the rest we don't know,
And never will as he says in his tweet storms.

This leaves us with Trump counselor Conway,

Whose stellar performances within the beltway

Are verbal works of awe, contemptuous of law,

Which we hasten to delete but hit…replay.

Air Quote

Oh Kellyanne! I'm your fan, your untold wonders to tell,
such virtuosity stuns sensibility, each languorous syllable
tumbles precisely. Primates gape at the press-conference belle—
microwaved, wire-tapped, alt-facted, walked-back—all spells
you cast with ease.

"Bad guy, sick dude," Trump's version of metaphorical whimsy
challenges not your range of hide-and-seek. Journalists' flimsy
complaints are easy to slide past, your meek peek-a-boo and pithy
repartee such a pleasure to behold—and your TV raillery!
Fox & Friends are pleased.

Facts fall from facts, what is true matters little, asserting power
vaingloriously, all aflutter with fame, a confluence of sour
impulses cheerfully delivered leaves me shivering as I scour
Breitbart for wisdom, an assault on reason no reason for our
hearts to seize.

And yet we watch and our hearts seize, as a climate of hoaxes
tornadoes our villages, and you, oh muse of delight, invoke
air quotes to explain away—happily, with a smile—what folks
know to be true. I'm your fan, Kellyanne, lovely blower of smoke,
fungible Trump tease.

The Koch Brothers' Rag

I got 40 billion

You got a buck

My influence is legion

Yours, well, you suck.

I dwell in shadows

Manipulate at will

Dark money knows

It flows uphill—

To senators and trolls

Hard to distinguish

Between 'em

Both pay for polls

And try to extinguish

Their latter day foes—

Yes, they try to extinguish

Their latter day foes.

I got 40 billion

You got a buck

My influence is legion

Yours, well, you suck.

Toxic Empire—
We're so-called.
Top polluter
We're not appalled:

There's big money
In dirty oil—
What's a little funky
Toxic soil

When I'm rich
And you're not.
Courts bitch—
Overwrought

Sniveling fools
In robes. Felonies?
So what, who cares:
We're Celebrities.

I got 40 billion
You got a buck
My influence is legion
Yours, well, you suck.

Dark money rules
I've heard it said
Plenty of fools
Have slept in my bed

Of Cash—
Billionaire crack
House, my stash
Safely stacked

In place—My
Drug is power
Used on the sly
To devour

Your young.
Water or air
Bones or lungs
I don't care

How it goes,
I'll extinguish
Your kids, my foes
A whim, a wish—

Extinguish them

All, one at a time
Or together, Dems're
Easy to demonize.

I got 40 billion
You got a buck
My influence is legion
Yours, well, you suck.

Wiretapped II (Revenge of the Brits)

I think the president's been very clear when he talks about this, and he
talked about it last night. So we talked about wiretapping, he meant
surveillance and that there have been incidents that have occurred.
>   —White House Press Secretary Sean Spicer

Twaddle.
>   —British Prime Minister Theresa May

Ominous, Sean Spicer, incidents have occurred—
the Trump Tower targeted with surveillance
so sophisticated we can't work out blurred
images or mechanisms, cameras or agents,
or something in the water, creepy crickets
along the baseboards, cockroaches masquerading
as coffee beans, fleas and midges with tickets
to spy, insectivorous recording and annotating
(Ivanka's bugged jewelry poorly communicating)—
or high-tech observances sold as mere
contrivances of luxury, polished leather shoes
(twelve hundred a pair) microphoned to hear
each presidential fart. Oh! What conspiracy hews
to Spicer's tart thoughts free-forming in press calls—
to follow his logic is to follow faux art: Of course it's
Obama, if not Russia or China, but lacking the balls
for true conspiracy, with neither whimsy nor wit
but unerring uncertainty, Spicer hies to a tall
one: the wiretappers were our allies the Brits.

Travel Ban Two-Step

What is our country coming to when a judge can halt a Homeland Security travel ban and anyone, even with bad intentions, can come into U.S.?

—Donald J. Trump

Just cannot believe a judge would put our country in such peril. If something happens blame him and court system. People pouring in. Bad!

—Donald J. Trump

"Federal courts are the worst!"—the president proclaims
loudly enough to burst through any inane chatter
from the left—"So-called judges cannot simply chain
up my Muslim ban, bereft of reasoning, nattering
on about the Constitution. We are imperiled, under threat,
damn refugees flow through unchecked at the border—
How dare courts step in front of my executive order?"

Courts in their measured way
Outlast the noise
Unswayed by bombast.

"No one has heard of these judges so-called, who fret
about nothing. They force exotic hijabs on Christian
sensibilities, say 'my bad' when extreme vetting
is banned, and otherwise fail to protect our nation

from Islam. The so-called will rot in the dustbin
of history; my name will not, emblazoned atop
a stunning, long-running, borderline malaprop wall!"

Judges in their chambers
Appalled at the idiot-king
Issue rulings that sting.

"I'm, like, a smart person"—Trump avers, blinking
back outrage—"No waivers for bad people, I know
their odors, their tears, their selections, their thinking
and none of them buys from my collection of ties! So
when badly dressed pour over our borders, Trump-tailored
Christians need our support and protection: Fashionable
Democracy I say! (And, by the way, I'll never be taxable)."

Courts counsel calm
Executive power has limits
For presidential dimwits.

Oligarch's Lullaby

Together, 27 White House officials had assets worth at least $2.3 billion when they joined the administration.

86% of Trump counties make less in a year than 27 Trump staffers are worth.
                                                      —*Washington Post*, 4/1/17 (no joke)

We must make our choice. We may have democracy, or we may have wealth concentrated in the hands of a few, but we can't have both.
                                                      —Louis Brandeis

My sweet child, don't despair
I'm not really your mother
Or your father, both away
At the Trump Cabaret.

Close your eyes, they are rich
You've no worries, perfect pitch
You'll live long, with no cares
You'll inherit your fair share.

Go to sleep, my sweet child
Wondrous blessed 'n' beguiled

One percent, it is true
Every penny is for you.

All for you, my sweet child
Just for you, God has smiled
All the rest, time for prayer
Their lowly lives to repair.

Close your eyes, wealthy sage
Gilded Age now comes of age
Your constraints, barely there
Never will be, billionaire.

Sleepyhead, time to drift
Sleep is nigh, sleep is swift
Machinations in your name
Soon enough you'll be to blame.

That's your fate, that's your lot
Noblesse oblige it is not
Ninety nine percent are fools
It's one percent that rules.

Go to sleep, be at peace
Passed to you a golden fleece
Wear it well, with righteous flair

You'll never be an au pair.

An au pair, not like me
My poor life of misery
From afar, now with you
Go to sleep, *adieu adieu.*

Guten Abend, gute Nacht
Mit Rosen bedacht
Ninety nine percent are fools
It's one percent that rules.

Mitch

Kentucky's mean spirit: he
    Shows us who's boss.
The Constitution? The Senate?
    His oath? All tossed.
No highfalutin, no circumlocutin:
    Mitch, what the fuck?
A burst vessel entombed in your skull
    Is a stroke of good luck.

The Deep State Conspires

The Word was not made flesh, Evangelist.
    That's really quite absurd.
As good Darwinians we must insist:
    'Twas Flesh that made the word.
                      —Robin Fox

The subway, dank and cheerless,
fills with my kind, suited, shod
in running shoes, compressed
cheek to cheek. Even, odd—
I mark them as we clatter
and stop at each platform—
my ongoing interior chatter
impossible to stop or deform
into another state of mind
as, arms stretched above, we grasp
slender silver branches, blind
to our up-from-the-slime past.

Doors open, my kind shuffles
forth, a peculiar hominid gait,
and, escalated in lines, we hustle
to the surface. Work awaits.
Black polished shoes replace
the small colors on our feet,

hum of computers, we brace
lattes against our chins and chat
idly. Athletes we are not. Hunters
we are not. I gather as a packrat
oddments to share with others.

I hide my true self. Office mates
see themselves in me; mirrored
thus I toil daily for the deep state,
turning lies to dust. Borrowed
ideologies I trust not to brighten
the path for tribal bureaucrats,
whose forlorn power tightens
nooses around loose autocratic
necks and jowls, a jugular squeeze
of devotion. Apparatchiks Unite!
my coffee mug proclaims, a tease
to those colleagues on the far right.

Unaware of Darwinian knowledge
I lightly wear—a kissing disease
of primordial heft and sacrilege—
my mates accept kisses and agree
their cheeks to turn and turn again,
rouged and warm to my lips. They
taste of secrets. I fumble my lines:

'twas flesh made words, I try to say,
genomes, garden gnomes, clandestine
twists that produced those evangelists
absurd in body and message and word,
and now, deep state, the kiss transferred.

The kiss transferred, that work begun,
I unravel presidential directives—
fallacies we take for truth—one by one.
Senior staff, amateurs all, selected
for loyalty, have the gall to pronounce
vast changes. We laugh into our
lattes. Simple to say, we countenance
no such changes and hold at bay hour
by hour communiqués and pressing
matters of state, we wink ourselves
silly, woo the press and our friends
deep underground, our facts subtended.

How deep do I go? Self-deception
to start: consciousness and language
conspire to pull apart apperceptions;
kin produce their share of anguish,
in-laws require payments in-kind;
faith mixes mischief with muscle
as adherents insist they are blind

to reason. Still, democracy muffles
these evolved sensibilities, buffers
civilization's fragile institutions,
and encourages science to progress
despite latter day Stone Age regressives.

Preserving *that* status quo
is how deep state I go.

The Vote

Stunned
left standing
in the rain
Hillary weeps
her sins
lost
to history.

The Royal Family

It always bothers me when members of a family, who have never
been elected, show up suddenly as official state representatives and
are treated almost as if they were members of a royal family.

—German Foreign Minister Sigmar Gabriel

Ivanka and Jared,
Eric and the other one,
think we are air-
headed simpletons,
zombiefied brain
dead citizen sources
of profit—their notion
of good governance?
Oh! Be not so crass
to ask nor look askance
at Ivanka's imported
shoes, built on the cheap,
sold without merit, self-
reflection or guilt, Trump
brand the hook, sourced
overseas, which means
(do not look!) by people

whose means and color
are like rich dark loam,
useful for growing, not
welcome at home.

Disdainful royalty
in painful heels
and pained smiles
play at charades.
What do they eat?
What do they wear?
What do they cultivate?
Why do we care?
A chilled soup,
a cocktail, a grey
suit, a white dress,
a banker, a style—
I confess my
own disdain and
rising bile at the
mess we inhabit,
the press unable
to make a dent or
scuff the veneer,
the royal sneer
especially well-

placed on I & J's
lips.

Each wanker who voted
by proxy for this risible
pair, each self-dealing
moneyed Wall Street
banker whose bulls and
bears leave us reeling,
each Chinese favor curried
and corrupt, each frightful
blue blazer and garish
red tie—the fakery, the
puffery, the bullshit, the
lies—each parade of ring-
kissers in a tidy line of
hopeful twits seeking aid
and given crumbs deftly
granted with a smile and
a royal thumbs up if you're
worthy and rich, each Russian
spy obscured by wealth and
fat ambassadors, each
new administrator intent
on rendering science as
a vat of tallow, turning

thought to muck, each

secretary—good God,

Rick Perry?—welcomed

as royalty to the dance no

matter how vacuous, how

hollow, each charmed

constituent struck stupid

with awe at the spectacle

of excess Jared and Iva,

spoiled fish that they are,

express as normal life, each

butchered sentence, each

gutted norm, each shared

value turned sour, each

amendment drained of

meaning, each imperiled

working class voter, each

river, each forest, alas, each

twisted tweet blast re-

tweeted ad nauseam if

stridently uncivil (who

follows such drivel?), each

deal to enrich the rich, capital

and political heft joined once

more, an old story in truth,

the poor and uncouth look

on as before, Jared and
Ivanka minding the store
so to say, like drunkards
or aristocrats on a bender
of self-love, the frivolity
of the super-wealthy
en plein air display—
    and now—
we watch with dismay
knowing we've been
bamboozled, lured with
false promises of greatness
and great fortunes to be
made, knowing withal
reality's mislaid by the
carnival barker himself,
the king of the deal,
the court jester, the elf.

Anon

Fearful of trolls,
pundits and bullies,
twittering twits
and TV personalities,
preferring evening quiet
and morning tranquility
I opt for simple
blessed anonymity.

Eight billion humans,
fertile and fecund, grace
our planet as it precesses
and wobbles its way
'round the sun, heedless
of its fleshy burden. Once
spun, each striding hominid
will be, anon, undone.

Some sooner, some later,
all in good time: imagine
the Chief Twitterpater
coiffed with foundation
well-spread on his cheeks

lying intestate upon a slab
of marble as we all marvel
at his fat inconsequentiality—

And bemoan our electoral
stupidity. We watch then with
glee his brats' headless battles
to control the brand that in
Trump-land was destined
to sizzle and fail, quizzical
courts uncovering bestial
corps and corpses of LLCs.

The fate of us all, towered
or small, spinning and wobbling
'round our sun, is to be forgotten,
just so. Politicians come and
go and the new White House cur—
cheerless confabulator, unrepentant
manipulator—will soon disappear.
Twenty years, a generation hence,
his life will have made no difference.

Made in the USA
Las Vegas, NV
24 September 2024

95712890R20031